Wing Chun:

The Ultimate Guide To Starting Wing Chun

© **Copyright 2014 - All rights reserved.**

This document is geared towards providing exact and reliable information in regards to the topic and issue covered. The publication is sold with the idea that the publisher is not required to render accounting, officially permitted, or otherwise, qualified services. If advice is necessary, legal or professional, a practiced individual in the profession should be ordered.

- From a Declaration of Principles which was accepted and approved equally by a Committee of the American Bar Association and a Committee of Publishers and Associations.

In no way is it legal to reproduce, duplicate, or transmit any part of this document in either electronic means or in printed format. Recording of this publication is strictly prohibited and any storage of this document is not allowed unless with written permission from the publisher. All rights reserved.

The information provided herein is stated to be truthful and consistent, in that any liability, in terms of inattention or otherwise, by any usage or abuse of any policies, processes, or directions contained within is the solitary and utter responsibility of the recipient reader. Under no circumstances will any legal responsibility or blame be held against the publisher for any reparation, damages, or monetary loss due to the information herein, either directly or indirectly.

Respective authors own all copyrights not held by the publisher.

The information herein is offered for informational purposes solely, and is universal as so. The presentation of the information is without contract or any type of guarantee assurance.

The trademarks that are used are without any consent, and the publication of the trademark is without permission or backing by the trademark owner. All trademarks and brands within this book are for clarifying purposes only and are the owned by the owners themselves, not affiliated with this document.

Table of Contents

What Is Wing Chun? 4

Who Invented Wing Chun And What Is Its History? 6

When Is A Good Time To Start Wing Chun? 9

Am I Too Old For Wing Chun? 12

What Are The Requirements For Training Wing Chun? 13

Wing Chun Techniques 28

The 3 Non-Negotiable Elements Of Injury Prevention In Martial Arts 40

Mobility Work Reduces Risk Of Injury For Fighters 45

In Defense Of Self: The Real Mental Value Of Self-Defense Training 48

The Power Of Patience 57

Work To Learn; Success Will Follow 60

Five Deadly Mistakes In Martial Arts... And Life 64

Planning To Fail? 67

You Don't Need To Be The Biggest, Fastest Or Strongest 71

WHAT IS WING CHUN?

Wing Chun is one of the most famous and revered styles of kung fu to emerge out of Southern China. Unlike the wide, sweeping, circular and often acrobatic-looking movements commonly associated with kung fu from Northern China (and seen in many movies) Wing Chun is more subtle, straight-forward, and linear stressing a philosophy of "economy of motion" and "no wasted movement." Because of its absence of circular movements, flashy kicks, and difficult acrobatic movements, it's an ideal martial art for any age and level of physical activity.

One of the primary reasons Southern Chinese martial arts such as Wing Chun evolved so differently from its Northern Chinese counterparts is due to environment. In Southern China there were many tight-knit cities with narrow streets and alleyways, far removed from the wide, sweeping landscapes of the North.

Because of this, southern styles like Wing Chun became more street-oriented, stressing narrow stances with quick, short bursts of power. This is why Wing Chun is often known as one of the first true "street fighting" martial arts, which also makes it one of the most practical for everyday self-defense even today.

Another aspect of Wing Chun is its focus on ending fights quickly by utilizing fast "chain punching" techniques, eye jabs, strikes to the throat and groin, strikes to knee joints, and clinching. By emphasizing to students the importance of rapidly closing the distance on your opponent with "forward intent", there isn't much dancing around and fancy footwork as you would see with a traditional boxer or kickboxer, as the goal of the martial art is to get the job done quickly and efficiently with as little exertion, effort, and wasted movement as possible, ensuring that confrontations are brought to a finalization immediately.

Due to this no-nonsense approach, Wing Chun is not a sport fighting style, but a quick, deadly, street style where anything goes as long as it wins the fight.

Perhaps one of the most famous practitioners of Wing Chun was the legendary martial artist Bruce Lee who trained under the now-famous grandmaster Ip Man (portrayed by Donnie Yen in the movie Ip Man) in Hong Kong. It was the principals, movements, and philosophy of Wing Chun that made up the bulk of Bruce Lee's unique style of Jeet Kun Do.

WHO INVENTED WING CHUN AND WHAT IS ITS HISTORY?

Because the history of Wing Chun was passed down verbally rather than through writing, there is no solid origin and there are also many conflicting legends as to who invented it and why. It is theorized that some of these stories were made up to protect the true origins of Wing Chun during times of war and conflict in which Shaolin temples were being destroyed and many martial arts practitioners were considered rebels.

However, one of the most prominent and prevailing stories of Wing Chun's origins is the story of Ng Mui and Yim Wing Chun. As the story goes, a female Abbess of the Fujian Shaolin Monastery named Ng Mui escaped the destruction of the temple by Qing forces and fled into the distant wilderness of the Daliang Mountains (on the border between Yunnan and Sichuan).

While in hiding she came upon a fight between a snake and a white crane. While observing the fight, she noticed the distinct variations of styles between the darting and dashing of the snake against the bobbing and weaving evasion skills of the crane.

After observing the fight, Ng Mui combined the lessons she learned with her years of Shaolin kung fu training to create a brand new style.

During this time, Ng Mui would often bring bean curd to the tofu shop of a woman named Yim Yee who had a daughter named Yim Wing Chun.

Yim Wing Chun was very beautiful, and a local warlord was trying to force her into marriage.

Ng Mui decided to teach Yim Wing Chun her new fighting style and she promptly used it to ward off the warlord.

Eventually, Yim Wing Chun married the man she loved – Leung Bok-Chao, and taught the style to him and he named the system after her – Wing Chun or "eternal springtime."

There are many variations of this same story, including one in which Yim Wing Chun challenged the warlord who was trying to force her hand in marriage to a boxing match. The challenge was, if she won, she didn't have to marry him. After she did beat him with her new style of kung fu, she married the man she really loved.

Regardless of whether or not the stories are true or which version of the story is fact, similar elements always come into play and that is the observation of the snake and the crane fighting along with the style being developed by a woman, which highlights how Wing Chun can beat larger, stronger opponents with minimal force.

The imagery of the snake and the crane is also important to Wing Chun, as it is representative of many of the hand movements, such as the darting and poking movements of Biu Sao (representative of a snake striking) along with the covering and diversion techniques such as Fuk Sao (representative of the crane).

One of the most interesting things about the history of Wing Chun is how it spread among those in the Red Boat Opera Company as a secretive style, taught only by those in "the know." The Red Boat Opera Company was a group of Chinese travelling opera singers who toured China from the late 1800s and early 1900s.

It is often theorized that the Red Boat Opera Company was actually a cover for Qing Dynasty rebels who would mask their kung fu training as stage tricks in order to cultivate their skills in secret and defeat government troops.

Ultimately it was Ip Man who began teaching Wing Chun openly in the 1950s in Hong Kong, which allowed everyday people (like Bruce Lee) to learn the martial art and spread it throughout the world.

WHEN IS A GOOD TIME TO START WING CHUN?

There's no time like the present. You don't have to wait until you have reached a certain level of physical activity or flexibility. Because Wing Chun is just as suitable for the young as the old, you can feel comfortable beginning Wing Chun no matter where you are in your life.

WILL I BE OUT OF PLACE?

When you come into class there are going to be people that know more than you. Don't let that worry you. You see, our Wing Chun students and teachers are family and everyone who sets food in the door is family as well.

Whether you have previous training in martial arts or the most physical activity you've done is climb the stairs to your apartment – you will fit in just fine in a judgement-free zone.

We strive to make you feel comfortable, to support you, and to help you understand both the techniques and philosophy of Wing Chun so that you can apply both the physical movements and its philosophies to your everyday life.

There's a saying in Wing Chun circles, "Wing Chun cannot be seen, it must be felt." Because Wing Chun is very subtle without any kind of flashy movements, it can be very difficult for someone simply observing it to understand what's happening as Wing Chun often LOOKS as though not much is going on.

That's why it's so important to feel Wing Chun – to understand the effects it has on your body when applied and also when you are training it.

Because of this, we don't allow people to simply watch a class, and instead encourage any new or prospective students to simply come in on an "open day" to train with students who will work patiently with you and explain the concepts.

IS WING CHUN SUITABLE FOR EVERYONE?

Absolutely – whether you're young, old, fat, thin, male, or female Wing Chun is perfect for you. In fact, out of all the various traditional martial arts – from Karate to Jiu Jitsu – Wing Chun is probably the least physically demanding, which is part of the beauty of this ancient martial art. It remains just as effective, deadly, and fast regardless of your physical state. Someone who can run five miles without getting tired and someone who is overweight with a bad back will both find themselves able to easily perform the same techniques with similar effect.

IS WING CHUN SUITABLE FOR THE DISABLED?

The short answer is – it depends on the disability. We have seen plenty of examples where those who are blind, have cerebral palsey, are wheelchair bound, and have other types of disabilities are able to effectively train Wing Chun in their own way. Because Wing Chun is not physically intensive and highly adaptable, it's safe to say that there are a large variety of disability types who can get a lot of out of training Wing Chun.

Let us know beforehand if you have a particular disability. We will do our absolute best to accommodate you.

AM I TOO OLD FOR WING CHUN?

If you're not too old to drive, feed yourself, make your bed, and shop for groceries then you're not too old for Wing Chun. The beauty of Wing Chun is how seamlessly it transitions with age. Someone who begins training in their teens can train just as intensely and with just as much skill in their eighties. Due to the philosophy of "no wasted movement" in Wing Chun, strikes and techniques do not rely on muscle strength, physical speed, and lots of cardio-intensive footwork. Instead, it relies on the ability to use the least amount of force for the largest amount of impact. Because of this, you spend more time training how to relax and NOT rely on strength or sheer physical ability within Wing Chun, which makes it perfect for older practitioners.

WHAT ARE THE REQUIREMENTS FOR TRAINING WING CHUN?

Leave your ego at the door, don't take yourself too seriously, allow yourself to make mistakes, and simply have the desire and fortitude to keep training the techniques. As is the case with any skill in life, you have to practice, put in the time, and remain consistent in order to learn.

However, if you have a difficult time taking instruction, you think you know better than the instructors, or your sole purpose is to get into physical confrontations, it's probably best that you don't train Wing Chun.

WHAT DOES A TYPICAL CLASS CONSIST OF?

A typical class will start with some light exercise and stretching to get your body warmed up. After that, we may start out with Wing Chun's first form (Sil Lum Tao), work on a few punching and kicking drills, or work on some pad drills with partners.

Each of our classes is hands-on and partner-oriented. We pair partners based on their skill level and often spend the bulk of a class period working on a particular technique in a variety of different ways in order to "drill" the technique into your mind, hone it, and ensure it becomes second nature.

DO YOU HAVE A GRADING SYSTEM?

Although traditional kung fu had no grading systems, we have since found it necessary to at least separate people based on their knowledge of Wing Chun. However, it should never be a student's goal to progress grade-by-grade simply for the accolades that comes with it. Because of that, we don't put a lot of emphasis on quick progression through our grading system and we do not think students should either.

Students progress in the grading system based on their knowledge of Wing Chun's principals, philosophy, and techniques. For example, anybody can learn the movements of the Sil Lum Tao form, but do they understand what the movements are for? Do they understand how to transfer energy into those movements? Can they name each movement and explain its applications?

To find more out about our grading system come try out a class and talk to one of our coaches.

DO I NEED TO BE AGGRESSIVE?

Whether you consider yourself an aggressive person or you consider yourself a passive person, the first goal of Wing Chun is to get you to relax, understand your movements both from a philosophical standpoint and a technical standpoint, and build you from the ground up.

After that, you will know how to use aggression and what levels of aggression are necessary in any particular situation – from friendly training with a partner to a street confrontation.

By first learning how to control yourself, your movements, and your mind, you will be able to utilize physical aggression when necessary.

However, when we train, the goal itself is not aggression and if you consider yourself someone who avoids conflict, you will not feel overwhelmed by the need to have an aggressive personality where none exist.

WILL I GET HURT IN CLASS?

With any physical activity there is a risk of getting hurt – the same is true for driving a car or walking down the street. However, unlike stepping into a boxing ring in which you can expect to receive blows to the face and torso, this will not happen in Wing Chun. Although sparring occurs, it is very controlled and full-contact sparring is only for students who have learned to control their strikes and have been training Wing Chun for an extended period of time.

However, the Wing Chun system does put an emphasis on strengthening and hardening the knuckles, forearms, fingers, and palm by striking hard surfaces such as bags filled with beans, buckets filled with sand, and wooden dummies (Mook Jong). This will inevitably result in bruising. The goal is to take it slow, hardening your bones little by little over time. So, although you will receive bruising, you will not result in any kind of debilitating injury.

DO I HAVE TO BE FIT TO START?

Absolutely not. The training regimens in Wing Chun will undoubtedly improve your fitness level to a certain extent, but that is not to say that training is arduous or strenuous. Aside from light exercises at the beginning of each class mixed with light pad work and sparring, Wing Chun training itself does not require a high level of flexibility or physical ability. You will not be throwing out high kicks, jumping, and running.

Because Wing Chun stresses economy of motion and no wasted movement, the goal is to exert as much power as possible with the least force. Because of that, Wing Chun is more concentrated on relaxing the body and the mind while understanding how to produce quick, short, explosive power shots rather than more complicated, cardio-intensive movements.

HOW LONG WILL IT TAKE TO GET GOOD?

This, of course, depends solely on the practitioner – your level of attendance and dedication, your willingness to understand the deeper notions and philosophies of the system, how much time you practice in your off time, and so on.

However, it's safe to say that, with regular attendance, the average student should be able to apply a range of techniques correctly and skillfully in about six months of training.

The Wing Chun system itself was designed to be learned quickly. Rather than relying on hundreds of various forms (such as other systems like Choy Lee Fut or Northern Shaolin) Wing Chun only has three short open hand forms, one wooden dummy form, and two weapon forms for a total of six.

However, just because the techniques within Wing Chun are simple and straight forward does not mean there aren't various layers. Although a student can learn to correctly apply technique within six months, learning the deeper meaning behind movements, learning to quickly adapt to surprise situations, and honing sensitivity skills such as Chi Sao and Lop Sao will take significantly more time.

WHAT ARE THE WING CHUN FORMS

Unlike other traditional martial arts including Japanese Karate's Katas and the sometimes hundreds of various forms present in popular Chinese kung fu styles, Wing Chun keeps it brutally simple. There are only three empty hand forms, one wooden dummy form, and two weapon forms.

Not only does Wing Chun not have a large number of forms, the forms it does have are short, simple, and do not require large, sweeping motions. In fact, arguably the most important fundamental form in the entire Wing Chun system (Sil Lum Tao) is completely stationary involving no footwork whatsoever.

The best way to think of Wing Chun's forms is to think of them as a "catalogue" of movements. In a sense ALL martial arts have forms. Take boxing, for example, the act of "shadow boxing" is something most boxers engage in. This is something they do to warm up, practice their techniques, and train when there are no bags or partners to drill with. Shadow boxing is simple – it allows the practitioner to utilize the common footwork, bobbing weaving motions, and the fundamental punches of boxing (jab, cross, hook, uppercut).

Much in same way as a boxer or Muay Thai practitioner or even a grappler will practice the fundamental techniques of their art in a solitary environment, so a Wing Chun practitioner will practice our forms. We do this to "drill" the most fundamental movements of the system in a solitary state for several reasons:

- To ensure the movements become second nature
- To understand each movement individually as part of a whole
- To remember the purpose of each individual movement
- As a free-flowing, meditative experience

Now that you understand a little bit about why forms are so important in Wing Chun, let's look at the six forms within the system.

EMPTY HAND WING CHUN FORMS

- **Sil Lum Tao (Little Idea)**

Although arguably the simplest Wing Chun form – as it is stationary and does not involve any footwork – Sil Lum Tao is also the most important Wing Chun form as it is the embodiment of the Wing Chun philosophy and the entire system's foundation.

From the outside looking in, Sil Lum Tao doesn't look like much. However, the importance of this form cannot be understated. It can be quick – taking two minutes or less – or it can be long taking 20 minutes or longer. It can be nothing more than a simple form to practice Wing Chun's fundamental hand movements, stance, and centerline theory, or it can be a deep, meditative energy practice (Qigong) in which one moves slowly, controlling the breath and sinking one's energy into the ground in a practice of "rooting."

In the form itself, you learn fundamental hand movements such Tan Sau (dispersing hand), Fook Sau (covering/prostrating hand), Wu Sau (protecting hand), Pak Sau (slapping hand), and more.

Because the form is stationary, it also trains your stance, strengthening your legs, and improving your balance.

- **Chum Kiu (Bridging The Gap / Seeking The Bridge)**

This is the second form in Wing Chun. Unlike Sil Lum Tao, Chum Kiu is not wholly stationary. And, unlike Sil Lum Tao where most of the techniques are done with one hand at a time, Chum Kiu gets both hands working together (along with the movement of the feet). Chum Kiu also employs some basic kicks (snap kicks).

The goal of Chum Kiu in "bridging the gap" is to train you how to quickly close the gap between you and your opponent, disrupt their structure, and throw them off balance while employing the many close-range attacks, elbows, and knees used in Wing Chun.

- **Biu Ji (Thrusting Fingers / Little Finger Pointing to The Moon)**

If you remember one of the central themes regarding the founding of the style of Wing Chun, in which the supposed creator Ng Mui observed a snake and a crane fighting in the forest, you can think of the Biu Ji form and its techniques as the striking fangs of the snake.

Biu Ji utilizes some of the most deadly open hand techniques in Wing Chun, namely the "stabbing fingers" that target the most vulnerable areas of a person such as their eyes and neck. You can think of turning your hand into a blade, or even a needle, and quickly and fiercely attacking.

Biu Ji is composed of both short-range and long range techniques complete with low kicks and sweeps. This form teaches elbow strikes and recovering from situations in which you've lost your "center line" during a fight.

There's an old Wing Chun saying, "Biu Ji doesn't go out the door." Often this is interpreted to mean that the form should be kept secret or that it should never be used if you can help it. The techniques used are for maiming and killing, especially if one begins learning pressure points.

WING CHUN WOODEN DUMMY FORM

The Mook Jong or "Wooden Dummy" is a fundamental training tool in many styles of Kung Fu, especially Wing Chun. Although there is only one wooden dummy form in Wing Chun, it has 108 movements and is rather complex.

The wooden dummy itself mimics a person (which is why it's sometimes called a wooden man) with two outstretched arms, one arm in the middle (mimicking a low punch) and one curved "foot" at the bottom allowing for leg kicks.

One of the fundamental purposes of the wooden dummy form is to train the practitioner to attack while being mobile – to move around the opponent while simultaneously attacking and defending, utilizing evasive footwork, kicks, and angling movements without sacrificing the center line.

The Wooden Dummy brings together all three of the empty hand forms and applies them to an actual opponent in which the force of your strikes is actually met with real resistance.

The other very important aspect of wooden dummy training is conditioning of the body or "iron body" techniques. By hitting the wooden dummy over time with varying degrees of impact, you your bones start to get small hairline fractures. When your bones heal, they heal stronger allowing you to hit the wooden dummy harder and harder without pain.

When practicing on the wooden dummy you build up your knuckles, palms, and forearms, effectively turning your arms into a weapon. Even after a few months of working with the wooden dummy, your knuckles, palms, and forearms will become stronger and "sharper." Hitting someone with knuckles that are conditions is much different than hitting someone with knuckles that aren't. Not only does it damage the person who is attacking less (because you have conditioned your hands and arms) it hurts your opponent much more.

WING CHUN WEAPON FORMS

Keeping with the trend of simplicity within the Wing Chun system, there are only two weapons trained – the butterfly knives and the dragon pole (staff). Unlike many other Chinese kung fu styles that employ a wider range of weapons training (spears, long swords, broad swords, and many incarnations and variations of these weapons) Wing Chun only concentrates on these two.

Now, many people now see absolutely no use for training something like butterfly knives or long poles. After all, who is going to be carrying around two huge knives or a 8 to 13 foot pole at any given moment? When are one of these items going to be lying around when someone is attacking you on the street?

Because of that – what is the point of training it?

The thing is, the likelihood of anybody carrying butterfly swords or long poles around when Wing Chun was invented and being taught in secret is also highly unlikely.

The reason these two weapons forms are trained has nothing to do with the thought that they should (or could) actually be used on a daily basis.

The reason they're trained is much more practical than that, which we'll look at now.

- **Baat Jam Dao – Wing Chun Btterfly Swords (Eight Cut Swords)**

The great thing about Butterfly Swords is how utterly diverse they are. They can be used to slash the enemy, but the backs of the knives can also be used to bruise, break, and thwart attacks by – for example – striking at the wrist. Historically, Butterfly Swords are known as Dit Ming Do (Life-taking knives).

The goal of the Batt Jam Dao form, aside from demonstrating the various parrying, slashing, and stabbing motions you can utilize with the knives, is to allow the knives themselves to become an extension of your forearms.

In reality. It gets you used to utilizing your empty hand techniques while holding a weapon. This prepares you to use a number of handled weapons from knives to short sticks without somehow abandoning the effectiveness and principals of your empty hand techniques.

By getting used to the knives being an extension of your arms, you can replace them with a number of objects.

- **Look Dim Boon Grun (Dragon Pole / Six and Half Point Pole)**

As previously stated, I can think of very few situations in which you would have access to a pole between five and 13 feet long at any given moment. So, what is the point of the dragon pole form?

First of all, I want you to imagine wielding a long pole that is around one inch in diameter. It gets heavy VERY quickly.

What's beneficial about this is how it strengthens your grip, your wrists, and your arms. It also improves your "driving force", which is your ability to quickly explode forward with immense, explosive power.

Training with the dragon pole in the Look Dim Boon Grun form dramatically improves your strength, stamina, grip, and explosive footwork, which translates directly into your empty-hand Wing Chun techniques.

WING CHUN TECHNIQUES

As already stated Wing Chun is a traditional Southern Chinese martial art, which was developed in the Shao Lin Monastery in the "Spring Temple", therefore the name Wing Chun means Forever Spring. Compared with other systems, it focuses more on restraining the opponent and lowering down the damage to the lowest degree.

The fundamental concept is based on 3 aspects:

1. Facing. When a person is performing the technique in a combat, he'd better make his whole body face the same direction. It is called "facing" since it means his body is not turning around. Facing can help the person concentrate his mind, and then use the whole body more efficiently. When facing is done properly, it can create a good position for striking.

2. Center line. It means that, from the top of his head to the end of his feet, it forms one line. The person should strike from his center line to opponent's centerline, as it is the shortest distance between the 2 fighters. In case of the same fist speed, the shorter the distance, the more probable to hit the target.

3. Straight. The reason the person needs to be straight is that he can release the power more explosively and efficiently.

Since the concept is as important as the technique, using the correct concept and being aware of full body positions can lead to a flexible body application.

Wing Chun technique consists of 3 hand forms:

    1. Xiu Lim Tao, also called Little Idea.

    2. Chum Kiu, also called Arm Seeking.

    3. Biu Jee, also called Thrusting Fingers.

For Xiu Lim Tao, there are a series of hand techniques as defensive moves.

The first is Tan Sau, which means Dispersing Hand. Tan Sau is one of the three pillars in Wing Chun techniques (Tan Sau, Bong Sau, Fook Sau). It is the first technique in the Wing Chun Character Sun Fist, and the most useful technique to combine with other techniques. To some extent, Tan Sau means loosening hand. While in Wing Chun, Tan Sau means to let the opponent's fist power diverge away from your center line along with the arm, so as to unload the power. It needs the use of the whole arm while the wrist needs to be straight. Any type of curve may hurt yourself. It is mainly used to lead to a direction or block the delivery of force upon meeting the force. When performing this technique, the person should put down his elbows. Tan Sau belongs to the passive not active technique as it is changed according to the opponent's striking variations.

The Tan Sau technique is performed like this:

1. Open with Yee Gee Kim Yeung Ma (this will be mentioned at end of the article).
2. Fist turns into palm;
3. Generate the power from end of elbow to finger, move palm from body center line and keep the palm heart upward, and the palm is in the supine position.

Instructional Video of Wing Chun Tan Sau:

https://youtu.be/Nj7Fv1Xrx9Y

A Demonstration Video of Tan Sau and Wooden Dummy Training:

https://youtu.be/qpdJmwwabyQ

The second is Huen Sau, and it means Circling Hand. It is a good technique focusing on wrist movement. It can be used against the strong power from your opponent and to change the position from inside to outside or from outside to inside. Tan Sau or Huen Sau can be combined together with other techniques.

Generally, after finishing every movement, it will go back to Huen Sau or Wu Sau as an ending.

How to do Hauen Sau:

https://youtu.be/WpvX2_bGD8U

https://youtu.be/MIYukp5_E8k

After Huen Sau, the hands are drawn back, and this action is Wu Sau, which is also called Guarding hand. While doing this, the person puts down the elbow and gathers the power at the wrist.

How to do Wu Sau:

https://youtu.be/DlXfRe6PLUQ

The next is Fook Sau; it means Subduing Hand. It is usually used to control your own space in the actual combat when a bridge is built. Generally speaking, when palm heart is down, forward, or towards left or right, it is Fook Sau. While holding Fook Sau and not moving, you can feel that the parts inside your arms and chest are relaxed. When the outside of your arms, the back of your body, and your legs are all stretched and tense up, that is one of the tips for power generation, which can impact the striking result.

How to Do Fook Sau:

https://youtu.be/GALCodpiim8

The last one is Pak Sau, which means Slapping Hand. The hand slaps from the center, and wrist and elbow at same time propel to the front of the chest. When 2 people are engaging in a combat, it is a way to slap the opponent away. There are two ways to generate power in Wing Chun: Long Bridge and Short Bridge, and Bridge refers to the forearm. It is Long Bridge when elbow is extending, while it is Short Bridge when elbow is curving. Pak Sau is in the range of Short Bridge for defence.

How to do Pak Sau:

https://youtu.be/rozXKxxWhAs

The followings are also the defensive techniques for hand form 2: Chum Kiu, its striking techniques contain Gum Sau, up, middle and down Bong Sau, as well as different kicks and steps.

Gum Sau means Pressing Hand. The move is to push hands to go downwards.

How to do Gum Sau:

https://youtu.be/StTuwMVTszU

Bong Sau means Wing Arm, one of the most important and variable techniques. It is to use one's body structure at different angles, in different directions, and by rotations to generate power, which can attain the effect of handling hardness with softness, and that is just using opponent's force to gain advantage. It can help you change the direction of opponent's strike. Its function is to take the advantage of body structure to defuse the frontal attack. Even a girl can resist a man's strong fist by using Bong Sau in case that she grasps this technique well since it can help shift between long distance and short distance or between strike and defence in a combat.

How to Do Bong Sau aka Wing Hand:

Video 1: https://youtu.be/mTnuVuqPYYc

Video 2: https://youtu.be/VQui_Me_j3Y

The next is Chi Sau, also called sticking hand. It is used to train students to follow the flowing force by sticking the opponent's hand and follow his hand movement. During the process, there is no need to speed up but just to follow concordantly. When performing this technique, ensure that the front arms and hands are submissive but not weak, dynamical but not rigid, and in the meantime keep the center line from moving.

How to do Chi Sau:

https://youtu.be/2TvvJcFLRcw

Biu Sau, also known as the Thrusting Fingers, belongs to the high rank striking skills in Wing Chun techniques. It is the hitting method which overturns the traditional technique by inheriting and developing the Siu Lim Tao and Chum Kiu. This technique requires the hit to drive small strength against big strength by borrowing the strength from all over the body. Biu Sau is always used in the condition that your opponent is stronger than you. It can be used to hit your opponent's soft spots such as eyes and neck by fingers. The fingers have to be locked, and what's more important is that the wrists need to be straight and locked. When this technique is performed, the wrist needs to be strong. Essentially, it means how to generate the explosive powers with your body parts, and they might be your fingers, palms, fists, arms, and elbows. In general, Biu Sau is a Wing Chun technique which includes short, middle, and long distance striking.

How to do Biu Sau:

https://youtu.be/7enzOxurYyM

The difference between Thrusting Hand and Thrusting Finger is not big. Thrusting Hand is always used to handle straight line or curve line attack. Firstly, it can be used to guard the inner gate. Secondly, it can block the opponent's hand movement to prevent it from touching any body part and finishing his punch. In general, it is one of the most efficient ways to control space.

Elbow is used by short-range techniques. The best attack point is its surface and back part. In order to generate explosive power, it needs to aim at the shoulder line, and try to use other parts of body, e.g. turning the hip to bring the shoulder line back to the center. Actually the destructive elbow power comes from the hip.

Then it comes to another concept called "Emergency Hand". In the real combat, not everything will go your way, and the simplest thing might be the most difficult thing. The Emergency Hand technique can help you recover, and it is a new element in Biu Sau, which can help your body return back to center again. As Wing Chun is a defensive art, once someone holds your hand, it will block your strike, so in this situation, you can use Pressing Elbow to regain control over him. The main targets of elbow can be head, face, and arms, and the strike can be from different directions: from the side, the back, not only from the front, and can be horizontal, diagonal and vertical. It brings you the advantage that you can use your elbows to protect you at different angles. The function of this technique is to change and adapt.

Wing Chun techniques focus on the space in front of the body. Once two people come into contact, the first skill to use is Asking Hand (sometimes also called Sending Off Hand). As you are standing there, and someone is beside you, you have no idea where the attack is coming from and where is being hit, but while feeling there is something getting close to your upper gate from one direction, you can extend your arms and hands fast with strength to cover your gate, while not extend your hands like touching something, so only done fast, it can be explosive.

The next concept is Long Bridge Grasping Hand. It is not just holding hand, and it needs to be fast and explosive instead. It is not limited to the hands, may also be the head and the arms. Grasping is aiming at keeping the space for you to strike, and the position will maintain your safety, so it is actually the control technique, which will lead to the next step -- strike technique, the Ginger Punch, to hit the sensitive parts of the body.

One of the famous striking techniques is the Lin Wan Keun, the chain punch. From the name you will understand it is continuous fist attack, which is very vigorous. With power from the elbow and straight line hitting again and again, you can always put your opponent in a position with no strength to hit back. Now this technique is already widely known as the representative of Wing Chun fist technique. The key point of this action is to keep fist relax and only grip tight at the moment of hitting, maintain the fist in a straight line while striking and hitting in the same position continuously, keep shoulders in balance, and lock the wrist, fist, and the front arm in the same straight line.

How to do Lin Wan Keun (AKA the chain punch)
https://youtu.be/LP4PnDjaAak

Furthermore, One Inch Punch also possesses a decisive status in Wing Chun fist system. One inch is so short, just as its name implies, so it needs the person to strive for the most explosive power at the short distance. The key point to control it well is the opportunity of acceleration. The right time to speed up is only when the relaxed fist touches the opponent's skin (garment), at same time the punch breaks out upon the most explosive force. The one inch punch actually is a martial art manifestation of learning and practicing internally and externally. Even though it seems to be simple and ordinary, it can be a fatal attack. A super Wing Chun fighter has the ability to break an empty box in an around 1-3 inches short distance.

Explanation of the one inch punch:
https://youtu.be/vbsaRhcnhuM

All the introductions mentioned above are the upper body movement, and here below let's talk about the rudimental technique -- Yee Jee Kim Yeung Ma, which is the most basic posture of bottom of body. The word Ma means horse, which originated from the ancient cavalryman who rides the war-horse. A good solider should always be united with his horse as a whole. Yee Jee means that the toe and heel form a Chinese character "二", the distance between the two toes has to be a little shorter than that between the heels. This gesture can bring strong adhering strength to the foot on the ground. When you perform Yee Jee Kim Yeung Ma correctly, the barycenter should be around 1 inch after foot center, and in the meantime the body weight should be allocated to the front and back of the barycenter, and the top body should face the center and the waist needs to be straight.

Yee Jee Kim Yeung Ma:
https://youtu.be/R5MBjRgbWUo

Wing Chun, as a whole, is a defensive system which focuses on the concept to help body release energy and recover the body to the center line so as to control space well. Every move is powerful and explosive. The philosophy of Wing Chun is very efficient, especially in a short range combat. The guarding principle is to use minimum time, minimum energy, and minimum body movement to achieve the best possible defensive effect.

THE 3 NON-NEGOTIABLE ELEMENTS OF INJURY PREVENTION IN MARTIAL ARTS

Injuries occur for many reasons and I am not going to take the time to explain every single possible scenario, as that would be impossible. Instead, I'd like to focus on three factors that need to be in balance in order to prevent injuries: flexibility, mobility, and strength. These three qualities are the foundation for anyone looking to become more athletic, from the seventy-year-old grandmother to the 22-year-old elite athlete. They are the base on which you build your success. When one of these three factors is out of balance, it makes a very inviting environment for an injury to occur.

Let's start with the easiest factor to address: strength. Strength is a relatively easy skill set to attain. A basic strength and conditioning program followed several times a week under the guidance of a trained professional can improve your level of strength quickly, especially if you already practice a sport that promotes the development of strength.

The second factor is mobility, which is the ability to move a limb or joint through a full range of motion with control. Mobility work is voluntary and requires strength to perform the action (flexibility is usually a more passive skill that involves static holds to elongate the body's muscles). Both mobility and flexibility are important skills for any athletic person to possess, but unfortunately the development of these skills is often neglected during training. The more mobile an individual is, the more easily and freely they can execute their intended task. Whether this is throwing a roundhouse kick, passing guard, or just picking up a bag of groceries, greater mobility will always equal improved performance.

Every person is going to have unique mobility issues. To combat them, it is important to meet with a professional, and also educate yourself on how to properly treat your specific condition. Some of the more common mobility issues I see frequently at the gym involve impingement of the hips and shoulders. Many martial arts place heavy demand on these joints and the muscles that surround them.

One great way to improve mobility is through myofascial release and the various exercises which are specifically designed to target the proper movement of a joint or limb. Below are two ways to increase the mobility of your hips and shoulders.

Myofascial release for the shoulder girdle
Start laying on your side with a foam roller placed above your hip. Slowly roll up towards your shoulder while applying pressure onto the roller. When you feel tightness, stop, take a few deep breaths, and rock side to side to loosen up the connective tissues. Then continue your way up into the armpit. Once you reach the armpit, slowly roll a few inches from side to side to grind out any tension hidden in surrounding musculature. Repeat on the other side.
Video: https://youtu.be/jRjreUQcTkQ

Myofascial release for the hip flexors
Start lying on the ground with either a lacrosse ball or a PVC pipe placed in the middle of your thigh. Slowly roll up towards your hip while frequently stopping to rock back and forth to grind out the tension. Once you reach the hip, roll onto your side

and apply pressure to the TFL (tensor fasciae latae) located between the front of your hip and your glutes.

The third factor is flexibility, which refers to the range of motion in a joint and the length of the muscles that cross the joints. The specific sport or activity you are focusing on will determine the optimal level of flexibility you need. Remember: flexibility should be treated as a goal and something to be trained and improved with time. If you're so tight you can't touch your toes, rhythmic gymnastics might not be the sport for you, but just because you are naturally tight doesn't mean you can never attempt a sport. It just means that additional care needs to be taken to participate safely. Below are two stretches that can increase the flexibility of the hips and shoulder.
Video: https://youtu.be/_MYGIfBhncI

Stretching the chest and shoulders

Start by placing your hands and knees on the ground with one elbow resting on a Swiss ball. Allow your chest to fall to the ground while reaching away from your center with the supported elbow. Think about creating separation in your shoulder socket while holding the stretch. Hold the position for 45 seconds, shake the arm out briefly, then repeat on the same side.

Stretching the hip flexors

Assume the same stance as you would for a split squat, with one knee resting on a pad for some added comfort. Flex your glutes and slowly press your hips forward while maintaining the contraction of the glutes. Hold the contraction for five seconds. Relax the glutes and allow the hips to fall forward. Repeat two or three times until the hips have ceased forward movement once the contraction is released.

Practice these stretches several times a day and see how your flexibility improves.

MOBILITY WORK REDUCES RISK OF INJURY FOR FIGHTERS

It's a good day whenever a study comes along that validates your own theories as a martial arts coach - not only because it always helps to have more science on hand, but also because it means that martial arts are getting the attention they deserves. One area that has long needed research, and is oft neglected by coaches and athletes, is the importance of mobility work for combat athletes. A recent [study in the Journal of Strength and Conditioning](#) was among the first of its kind to look at the injury prevention needs of martial artists.

In the study, researchers used the functional movement screen (FMS) to determine the mobility and balance weaknesses in fighters. While they acknowledged that the FMS itself might be understudied for martial arts, they provided support for the strength of FMS across a wide variety of sports, and indicated that the movements covered in the test related to many performed in martial arts.

As a martial arts coach, my one reservation has been that the mobility work for the fighters is typically added on top of their present routines on four days of the week. So if the athletes did their specific martial arts training and strength and conditioning work already, they were advised not to change it. This is a good thing because it mimics the real world in which a fighter isn't going to halt everything to perform mobility work. However, the downside is that many fighters are close to overtraining, or actually overtraining, for much of their careers.

In this study, the intervention was proved effective. The researchers were looking for a score higher than 14 on the FMS and any asymmetries between muscle groups. A score above 14 means reduced risk of injury, whereas below or at 14 means an 11x greater chance of injury. Athletes who have a score above 14 but also have asymmetries between muscle groups are 3x more likely to be injured.

Clearly, this has major impact for fighters.

Before the intervention, the average score for all participants was 13.25. After just 4 weeks, the score for the intervention group climbed to 15.17, out of the danger zone, and again up to 15.33 for week 8, showing a sharper rise during the first month.

Assuming the standard FMS is an effective screen for fighters, it turns out that mobility and symmetry work (not in the bodybuilding sense), are excellent ways for fighters to prevent injuries. Of particular note, work on the shoulders and hips seemed to be critical. Adding this work into a fighter's routine can help improve performance and the length of his or her career.

IN DEFENSE OF SELF: THE REAL MENTAL VALUE OF SELF-DEFENSE TRAINING

Before I found martial arts, I was never a joiner of fitness classes, preferring the freedom to do my own thing, run in my own direction. My martial arts journey started with a once a week, eight-week course in December 2008. It was difficult to say the least to commit to an 8 class series - to make my own commitment, for something I wanted to learn; to put my desire first; to show up and not let other events overtake; to defend Monday nights from 5:30pm – 7:00pm, for 8 weeks. I had to defend against my need to put others needs first, to put myself in second place.

When I first started I was in physical therapy for a running injury. My pelvis was tilted back and to one side, giving me a false short leg. I couldn't bridge and turn to the left side to save my life. My core was weak. I was overweight. I looked older than I was. I was trying to get back in shape and was training to do a triathlon in the summer, and thought learning some self-defense skills would be helpful when training alone on the trails.

2008 proved to be a challenging year. Not only was I in physical therapy, but I was in mental therapy, too. Turns out I wasn't going to just learn physical self-defense techniques and walk away at the end of an 8 week course. Turns out I was actually on a journey we'll call "In Defense of Self" - a defense of health and fitness, of spirit, of happiness, an integration of mind and body. A self that needed to be recovered, found, dusted off and put back together.

Definition: Self-Defense
1. Defense of oneself when physically attacked
2. Defense of what belongs to oneself

Perhaps the second definition should be listed first. You need to know what belongs to you – your space, your body, and your mental or emotional status – in order to be able to defend it. You need to believe in your self-worth in order to defend yourself. You need to know it is not okay for others to take from you – whether it's something physical like your wallet, or something more intangible like your motivation and dreams.

As I continued to sign-up for 8-week session after 8-week session, it became something to hold on to. I learned to escape all the headlock holds, wrist grabs, and throat grabs. How to block a punch, how to clinch, how to fall and get back up again. I started to figure out how to move my body. I figured out I had a body. And my body wasn't the enemy. Having spent so much time with sports injuries, chronic sinusitis, and endometriosis, I had dissatisfaction in and distrust of my body. It did me no good and did nothing but let me down and cause me pain.

But something crazy happened. I reclaimed my body as a partner. These hands, these arms, this bridge, this twist, and I could toss someone off of me. I could control my limbs, my core, and the space around me. It was possible – I could have physical say over what could happen. My body was no longer the enemy, no longer a constant source of disappointment, but a reliable partner.

Physical Training vs. Mental Training

The physical body and physical training of martial arts techniques are only part of the equation. The mental aspect is perhaps even more difficult to train.

I'd propose that physical training is in fact significantly easier. Lift this weight 10-20 times, with sets, twice a week and you will see a difference. But change a thought pattern you've relied on for 15, 20 years, or more? That is a significant challenge.

Martial arts taught me to feel or, rather, to connect the mind and body. To balance my strengths and weaknesses, to see when strength in one context became weakness in another context. I apologized for the first two (okay five) years of martial arts to my partner - first out loud, then to myself, and then just with my actions. Holding back there, letting up there, feeling their pain, or discomfort. Identifying with their pain, discomfort, their ego, their trying to hang onto themselves in a bad position. Recognizing my own symptoms of pre-panic in others.

I've had to practice focusing on my game, to be what feels to me a little selfish; to go for attacks and dominant positions, and to trust the other person to take care of their own mental and emotional status. They are here to train and fight and don't need me to take care of them. In fact, it takes away from their training and does them a disservice. They, too, need to practice not escaping to a safe mental place when stuck in a tough situation, but to stay in the room both emotionally and mentally and to tough it out. They too need opportunity to manage their ego.

These mental aspects can be trained and you need to seek out the tools that work for you. I've been working on this aspect the past 6 months or so. I got two smart bits of advice that really helped me make progress.

First – Do a Self Check: Do a self-check before entering a situation, whether it be a sparring match or a difficult conversation at work. What is my mental and emotional status? What am I feeling? What in essence am I bringing into the room, the match, or the conversation? When I leave the room, the match, or the conversation, I should be leaving with those same things. I don't need to take anything from the other person with me; I don't need to take their frustration (it's theirs, not mine), their personal angst, or their workload. My wise friend Mark says, "don't be greedy with other people's problems." This bit of advice has helped me immensely to defend my self and not let it be consumed by others. Not that others ever ask for me to do that, it's just a bad habit that needs to be broken.

Second – Protect Your Energy: The second bit of advice was from my acupuncturist. Essentially, I needed to protect my chi, protect my energy. I did this by imagining a protective shell around my core before slapping hands for a match, or before a difficult conversation. They are them; I am me.

Stop Being Too Nice
This being "too nice" aspect has other ramifications for self-defense. Too often women are taught to be nice, to not offend, to not potentially hurt others feelings. This can cause issues that can actually put you in danger. In a parking lot, or when someone comes to your door, you might ignore intuition or let someone get closer than you should, because you are being too nice. It is hard work to undo this lifetime of training. I have finally learned I don't have to open the door just because someone knocks on it.
This is similar to the weak no. Controlling people look for the weak no. They push the limit to override your decision. This is an aspect of self-defense and martial arts that is completely mental and but can be

trained with practice just like physical self-defense. This is well covered in *The Gift of Fear by Gavin de Becker* and should complement martial arts training.

Believe Your Self-Worth
A key to self-defense is belief in your self-worth. Self-worth is different from self-confidence. I can have boatloads of confidence in my abilities, my brains, or other attributes. Self-worth is different. It's deeply internal and hard to see, it's an internal nugget, whereas self-confidence radiates outwards. Self-worth says you are worth defending.

When we teach martial arts to teenagers, it always brings a lump to my throat to talk about self-worth. To tell them they matter for more than their looks or who they date or how perfect they are in school, but for what they as individuals have to offer the world. It's a precious commodity that can easily slip away. Self-worth says you are worth defending – in more than one way, from more than just physical danger.

Self-worth says –
- You are worth eating healthy

- You are worth the time it takes to put on your running shoes
- You are worth the time it takes to seek out health care
- You are worth taking a moment to breathe deeply
- You are worth having your ideas heard and your opinion considered
- You are worth not losing yourself to someone else

I get asked, "Have you had to use what you've learned in your training?" I used to say no, not since I've learned it but I could have used it in the past. Now I have a new answer. "Yes, every day, every day I use what I've learned in self-defense - *in defense of self.*"

My goal now is for other people, the people who need it most, to find an open door to martial arts. I'm not worried about the field hockey players, the rugby players, the has-been high school jocks who find their way into the dojo. They'll do just fine. I want the ones who aren't quite sure who they are or why they are there, but have an inkling that somehow it matters they have taken that step to walk in the door and onto the mat. That somehow they matter... and are worth defending.

THE POWER OF PATIENCE

In society today, one of the most challenging aspects of a person's daily routine is having patience. We live in a world filled with daily "instant gratification," and being able to post-pone the pleasure of getting what you want right now, isn't on the top of the list for most people.

Imagine if you couldn't use your credit card to buy those shoes you want at the mall earlier or if you had to wait months to save up the money for a down payment on that new car at the dealership. For a lot of people, this feeling of "delayed-gratification" isn't pleasant. Instant gratification is rewarding, and brings a sense of satisfaction and accomplishment.

However, it doesn't leave room for long term plans. Having patience means having the ability to wait for something without getting angry or upset. Let's take a look at why having patience can be powerful.

Great accomplishments take time
The most important moments in our life usually don't happen overnight. Many days, or years, of

practice and effort must be put in to be able to accomplish any big goal. Imagine a person starting his or her own business. Without the patience of dealing with all the challenges that come up in the beginning of any new business, that person would quit and move on to something easier. No great business happens instantly. Having patience gives the owner time to get everything running properly so the main goal of being successful is attainable.

By not taking a small piece today, you have a bigger piece tomorrow

Imagine a person trying to lose weight by going on a diet and working out. If every day that person gave into the "instant gratification" of eating that Big Mac or skipping the gym to see a movie, will they be successful in their weight loss goal? Of course not. It takes a daily effort of doing the right things, like eating good food and getting the proper exercise to lose weight. With patience, a person knows that each day they will become closer to their target weight goal if they give themselves time and choose delayed gratification over instant enjoyment.

Patience gives life to your vision

Everyone has a vision of where their life is headed and patience is the key to getting there. A student who wants to become a doctor knows that he or she must go through years of schooling before being qualified. An athlete knows that they must dedicate years of practice in the gym before ever becoming a professional athlete. Whatever path you choose, you must have patience to put in the work, to make it through the down times, and know that one day your vision will come true.

WORK TO LEARN; SUCCESS WILL FOLLOW

In this day and age, society is focused on results and accomplishments. "Who has the best degree, or who has the highest position in a company, tend to classify where someone is at in life and why they are successful or not.

In martial arts, some people get into training because they want to make money or achieve some level of fame. They go to the gym simply to improve their skills, so when they fight they can win some money and brag to everyone they know that they're a cage fighter. Although making money and wanting to become famous is a worthy goal, having this mindset can be challenging for many reasons. Just like any job when you are very motivated by money or status, your passion will be strained when faced with adversity. Those are the times when the majority of people abandon their goals.

Bestselling author of "Rich Dad Poor Dad," Robert Kiyosaki, sums it up nicely when he says, "work to learn not to earn." What he means is when starting out in any profession, it's a lot healthier approach if you start out thinking, "what skills can I learn from this job" or "how can this job make a positive impact on my life?" This opens up your mind to look for answers to those questions, and it keeps you motivated to make it through when times get tough. If one thing is certain in life it is that we will be faced with many challenges. It's how we respond to those challenges that decides whether we will be successful or not.

Back in 2004, I was 16 and remember having one of the biggest setbacks of my life. At that time, I already started competing in amateur competitions and compiled a 5-0 record and was doing very well. My confidence was high from the results of winning my fights. I thought nothing could stop me.

My next bout was scheduled for the lightweight title in southern England. Leading up to the fight, I knew my opponent was a dangerous submission fighter and was choking out all his opponents in the first round. Instead of having the mindset of "training to learn and become better," I only thought about how I was unbeatable and just wanted to go out there and win. Learning would have to take the back seat because winning was on my mind. The fight ended with me getting caught in a submission in under a minute of the first round. Even though I knew exactly what the opponent was going to do, I couldn't stop it. Emotionally I was devastated and my confidence was badly shaken. Driving home after the fight I remember thinking, "what the hell happened?" Looking out of the car window on the way back to my home, I drifted into feeling sorry for myself and wondering, "how did everything feel so good, now feel so bad?" As a dedicated athlete, losing is one of the most painful experiences that most people wouldn't understand. When you pour you heart and soul into something and still come up short, it's not a pleasant experience. After a couple of days, I decided to snap out of the feeling of losing and decided to do something about it.

As I searched for answers while retracing my steps into that loss and the fight day itself, I discovered that I got away from a fundamental lesson - "I stopped training to learn and was only focused on results of wanting to win." By doing so I shut my mind off from learning the techniques to become better, and more importantly, I disabled my passion and motivation from having fun and enjoying the process of being a fighter. This lead me to not being relaxed in the fight and getting caught in a submission that I knew was coming. After losing, I made a choice to become a student again and always put learning before results, which lead to much success in the cage and going on a 10+ fight win streak.

Before looking at the money or results, you will get a job in life whether you're a martial artist, a student trying to become a doctor, or a clerk at a supermarket. It's important to ask yourself, "what can I learn from this profession that'll make me a better person?" A lot of times, the answers are right there in front of you. Putting learning before results keeps you in the right mindset to become happy and successful at whatever you choose to pursue.

FIVE DEADLY MISTAKES IN MARTIAL ARTS... AND LIFE

What does it take to be successful, not just in martial arts, but also in life? Not only is it important to focus on positive daily practices, like exercising and having a great moral compass (honesty, integrity, fighting spirit, etc.), but it's equally as important to understand the daily "sins" that could lead to ultimate defeat in life.

I use the word "deadly" in the title, because these mistakes are as serious as one can get in day to day life.

Mistake #1 – Closing your mind off from further learning
Everyone is constantly growing, one way or another. From birth, we are physically changing from infant, toddler, teenager, etc. We are growing mentally as well.

Realizing you never know enough and always have a lot to learn is one of the best mindsets you can have, as long as you're striving to learn more each day. You have something to learn from everyone, but it's best to learn from those that are on a path you want to be on. This can be difficult. Closing off your mind will leave you susceptible to whatever your environment is teaching, which is usually not a good thing. There's an old saying: "once you stop learning, unpack your bags, because you'll be there for a while." When we keep our mind open and looking for knowledge, we control our path and the destination we are headed for.

Mistake #2 – Not taking care of our bodies
Eating crappy foods and never exercising is a recipe for physical disaster, such as cancer, heart disease, and diabetes. Our bodies are our temple and we must respect them. We do so by exercising daily and eating nutritional foods like fruits, vegetables and good supplements.

Mistake #3 – Lying and Cheating
Lying and cheating will end up nowhere. Even though you may be able to fool people temporarily, in the long run people will catch on to your nature and want nothing to do with you. You will eventually be left all by yourself, with nothing but the lies and

cheating to keep you company. Nothing is worse than someone who doesn't keep their word or tries to cheat their way through life. AsAl Pacino says in the classic movie Scarface; "all I have in this world is my balls and my word, and I don't break them for nobody!"

Mistake #4 – Not having any goals
Goals give you direction and motivation in life! Without them, you're similar to a sailing ship adrift at sea. A lot of times the first step to success starts with writing a list of goals about what you want to accomplish in life, and small goals to take steps getting to your bigger goals.

Mistake #5 – Never Giving Back
When someone doesn't give back, it leaves an emptiness in their heart and stops them from feeling the ultimate thrill in life, which is making the world a better place!

Are you making any of these mistakes in your life? If you are, correct yourself now and make goals to get on the right track.

PLANNING TO FAIL?

No matter how much it may seem otherwise, people have control over their own destiny. Everything is attainable with the right life plan.

Successful people are the ones who turn obstacles into challenges to be overcome and life lessons to be learned. Successful people also usually have a clear map of what they want to achieve and how to get there. Those people obtain success by making the right choices in their careers and personal lives on a daily basis. Conversely, certain individuals make the same mistakes over and over again, which ultimately lead them to failure. Those are people who are presented with every opportunity in the world, and yet still end up in the same situation. This is largely due to attitude. Life is made up of the choices we make on a day to day basis, whether we notice it or not.

One inspiring quote by Benjamin Franklin is, *"if you fail to plan, you are planning to fail!"*

Here are 3 mistakes that can guarantee failure.....

The wrong people around you:
The company you keep affects the decisions you make and the direction you take. Surrounding yourself with people that are bringing you down every day by telling you to skip class or not go to practice will not put you any closer to your goal. When I was coming up as a martial artist, I knew my chances of success would be higher if I distanced myself from people who weren't pushing me to be the best person I could be. I chose to have friends, family, and coaches that wanted to win with me, so they all supported the dreams and plan that I had. We all help each other in work and in life all the time!

Having a weak belief system:
Your belief system is that tiny voice in your head, and the feeling in your gut, that tells you that you can or can't do something. Every single person has control over their own beliefs. It is extremely hard for many people to understand. So it is very important to make sure you are developing a strong, sound, robust belief system every day.

If you are saying to yourself every day, "I will never lose weight" or "I will never be happy," is reinforcing a weak belief system and is guaranteeing that you won't lose weight or ever be happy. To shape your beliefs, it is always important to observe your attitude, ensuring you keep a positive attitude, and believe in your gut that everything will work out (because 99% of the time it does). This will ensure that when problems arise you will knock them down, rather than letting them confirm your existing negative views about the world.

Never taking action:
In martial arts, everything is about taking action. Every day, if you don't wake up and take action by going to the gym or eating right, the chances of failure increase. By not making an effort on a daily basis, you ensure defeat. It is always important to work hard at your craft so you can obtain your goals.

Not making these mistakes can help you steer clear from many roadblocks that you may encounter in life. Surrounding yourself with positive people, checking your belief system, and taking daily actions will build the foundation for a happier life. Moreover, they are additive: by keeping the wrong people away and the right people around, you will be able to draw motivation and help from a strong support network. Developing a rigorous belief system each day will give you the power to get through some of the toughest circumstances life throws at you. Taking action each day towards what you want out of life will ultimately lead you to success. Each one will help build the other. Encouraging people will help you develop an optimistic belief system and encourage you to take action. Having a positive belief system will allow you to take action, and to believe that you are worth being around good people. And taking action will introduce you to more supportive people and reinforce your developing belief system. This is precisely how life becomes what we make it. It is vital to ensure your plan is headed in the right direction and not the wrong one. So my question is... are you planning to fail?

YOU DON'T NEED TO BE THE BIGGEST, FASTEST OR STRONGEST

I have never been the biggest, fastest or strongest. I most definitely know that, but you don't have to tell me.

There were always athletes that were better than me in the gym, but my dad always told me "never walk out the gym, hustle all the time. You never know who's watching". Isn't that the truth.

I wasn't a big guy, so the odds were stacked against me every time I went in there. I knew I couldn't throw the others around using my natural strength; I had to find a workaround. I had to put in the extra hours of cardio and all the extra time spent perfecting technique. Lessons and traits I will never forget.

Years after my last time in that gym, what I learned still helps me to this day. Cue another one of my dad's sayings, "If you are going to do something, make sure you do it right". From attempting to maximize my ability in the gym to getting the best out of my team in an office setting, I only have control of what I can control. No one can stop me in how far I wanted to go in athletics or in the business world. I came from a town of less than 150,000 people in northern England.

Winning and losing keeps you on an even keel. Just as you perform with your teammates in the gym, working in a team setting allows to you to productively work side-by-side with your co-workers on a daily basis. In the office, in the gym, on the field, or the court, you succeed together and fail together. It makes you a stronger person in the end.

To this day I continue to overachieve, if you want to call it that. From moving nearly 200 miles to work in a new city where I didn't know one single person, to creating a website and business that that focuses on teaching people like yourself the skills to be better in their Martial Arts. I want to continue to reach new levels of success. Why? Because it shows that anyone from any walk of life can achieve anything they put their mind to and are prepared put the work in to make it a reality. What can you do to ensure you're on the right path?

Stand out from the Crowd

If I were to give words of advice to any athlete or anyone in any position (work, sports etc.), it would be to stand out from the crowd. Make a difference in whatever role you may be in. Stay that extra hour at work, take an extra swing, run that extra lap, help someone who cannot help themselves. It all counts in the end. In addition, you never know who is watching. Just as I mentioned previously, scouts, supervisors, fans and co-workers will all take notice of what actions you take. This isn't anything new, but I do think it's a lost art in an age where people take things for granted more often than not. Taking a shortcut should never be an alternative.

Trust in your abilities

Only you can determine what you can and can't do. Being undersized in any sport is tough. Was I the most talented? Of course not. Was I facing athletes who were bigger, faster and stronger? You bet. I had to know in my heart and my mind that I was as good or better if I wanted to move forward. Trust in your abilities and don't let any type of negativity bring you down. You alone are ultimately responsible for the end result.

Believe in yourself

Pretty straight-forward. A lengthy description isn't required. Your abilities will only take you so far, but it's the unwavering belief that you belong. Have the confidence that you know you CAN do it. Can't is not an option.

Made in United States
Troutdale, OR
01/24/2025